barbican life history architecture

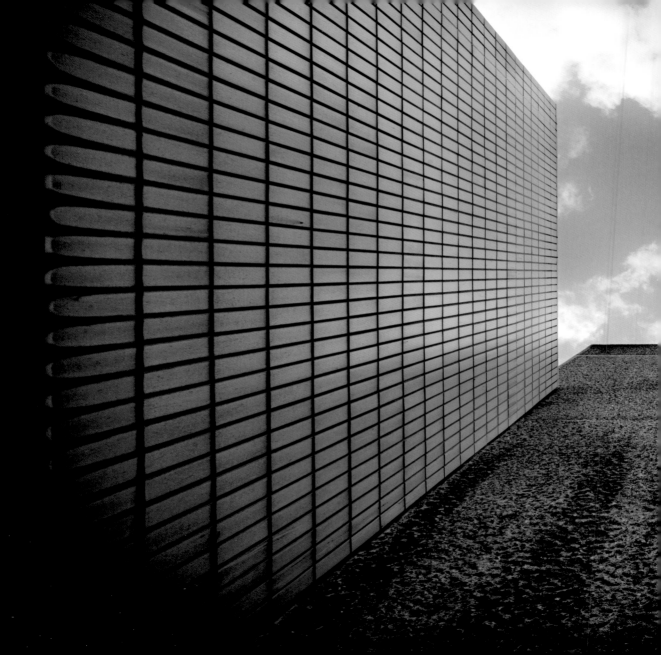

barbican

life history architecture

Edited by
Jane Alison and Anna Ferrari

Lakeside, Barbican.

Foreword

2014 marks 60 years since the architects Peter (known as Joe) Chamberlin, Geoffry Powell and Christof Bon were first approached by the City of London Corporation to act as consultants on the reconstruction of the Barbican. All three architects were in their early thirties. Eventually, Chamberlin, Powell & Bon landed the staggeringly ambitious commission to build what was to become a truly utopian piece of urban planning. Lengthy discussions were held in the City, the financial heart of London, to decide whether to go ahead with the radical reimagining of an area almost completely flattened in the Blitz. The Court of Common Council passed the proposal only by the narrowest of margins.

The Barbican is home to over 6,000 residents and to a multidisciplinary arts centre which opened in 1982. It was 30 long years in the making. Always controversial, the Barbican's massive architectural statement still divides opinion. As an estate, it is characterised by Le Corbusier-inspired hand-chiselled concrete, the wrap-around horizontal residential blocks which float like ocean liners above the city, high-level walkways and ramps, and the three 43- and 44-floor residential towers, which were for a long time the tallest in Europe, their distinctive serrated edges a landmark on the London skyline. Now the penthouse suites and varied apartments and houses on the estate are in huge demand; families, artists, architects and designers make up a growing proportion of residents. Many seek to live here for the convenience of proximity to work, the security of its safe haven in the City and the peace found here amid the carefully landscaped and lovingly maintained gardens and lakes. Fittingly, the Barbican Estate was listed by English Heritage as being of Grade II architectural significance in 2001.

The idea that the arts as well as culture and education would be a central part of this new urban quarter was there from the start in nascent form, but it developed and grew as the scheme progressed. The Guildhall School of Music and Drama was integrated from the beginning, and, originally, their facilities were also intended for use by other performing bodies. When the Royal Shakespeare Company and London Symphony Orchestra were invited to become resident companies in the mid-1960s, the planners realised that they would have to excavate down to accommodate the size of auditoria and facilities (including the theatre fly tower) required to service such prestigious stakeholders. The late insertion of such grand but hidden venues into an already defined site resulted in the lack of an obvious entrance – something remedied in the 2006 refurbishment by Allford Hall Monaghan Morris (AHMM).

Over the years, the Barbican's architectural reputation has grown in importance as its special variety of 'brutalist Modernism' is increasingly studied and admired. Just recently the internationally acclaimed architect Frank Gehry brought his students from the Yale School of Architecture, in New Haven, Connecticut, to study the Barbican and respond to its buildings.

Equally, at the Barbican Centre we have greatly developed our arts programme: today the Centre – owned and principally funded by the City of London Corporation and supported by a wide variety of private and public funds – is internationally renowned for its world-class programme of music, theatre, cinema and visual arts. Between 2012 and 2013, our two theatres, concert hall, three cinemas, art gallery and Curve gallery attracted a combined audience of over a million people, of which nearly 200,000 attended free events.

An ever greater number attend the commercial events which fill the Centre's spaces with richly varied celebrations – from weddings to graduations and conferences. We stage over two thousand arts events per year, many by our resident orchestra, the London Symphony Orchestra, as well as those by our associate companies, such as Michael Clark Company and Cheek by Jowl.

We have fostered creative alliances with our neighbours, the Guildhall School of Music and Drama (whose fine new building at Milton Court has, like the Barbican's new cinemas, added to the attractions of the area); and a joint department of Creative Learning takes the activity of the Centre and School beyond the walls of the City. World-class arts and learning are central to our mission, and as a National Portfolio Organisation funded by Arts Council England we are able to serve communities beyond the Square Mile. The result is that we have become a valued part of East London's thriving cultural life.

Finally, we are working with the City and our nearby partners, including the Museum of London, to create in this unique area a cultural hub that radiates out from the Barbican in all directions, thereby connecting us with the vibrant artistic communities in Clerkenwell, Shoreditch, Islington and beyond. With the arrival of Crossrail in 2018 the area will be better connected than ever, able to attract new audiences to discover and love the arts by bringing them into contact with outstanding artists and performers. We want Barbican to be truly accessible and welcoming: a place that produces experiences of the highest quality, which inspire our many audiences, and that offers arts without boundaries.

Nicholas Kenyon
Managing Director

Jane Alison
Head of Visual Arts

Brass handrail,
Barbican Theatre.

Theatre, Barbican Centre.

Concrete City: Chamberlin, Powell & Bon's Barbican

Otto Saumarez Smith

The Barbican is the most significant piece of post-war city building in Britain. Here was a rare occasion where the post-war architectural imagination was not hampered by penny-pinching, but was given full expression. The effect is staggering, striking a visitor with its bloody-minded ambition, its immersive scale, its often bewildering multi-dimensionality, its elemental geometries and its sculptural grandeur. The Barbican gloriously overturns the common Modernist failing of conceiving buildings as isolated objects in space. The architects fused the various components of this vast project into a theatrical townscape composed of multiple interlocking spaces on varying levels. Over 35 acres, the Barbican contains a range of different-sized flats housing up to 6,500 people, coupled with a host of cultural, recreational and educational amenities. Famously disorienting to navigate, the Barbican demands to be explored. It reveals incrementally its multitude of spaces, from the enclosure of a small courtyard, to the sublime scale of the three towers with their jagged silhouettes, to the seemingly precarious bridge and slab block rising like a Leviathan on giant pilotis, to the secluded calm of the elegant and formal water gardens.

When the last stage of the Barbican was finally completed in the early 1980s, decades after it first began to be planned in the 1950s, it was in a world very different from that in which it had been conceived. The Barbican was anathema to the architectural culture of the early 1980s. On completion, it was understood as the last expression of the largely discredited master plans of the Modernist pioneer Le Corbusier, whose Ville Radieuse from the 1920s had envisaged the total rebuilding of Paris with tower blocks set in parkland. The ideas of Le

Corbusier, however, formed only one ingredient in the rich mix of influences and ideals that informed the architects of the project, Chamberlin, Powell & Bon (CPB).

The three main members of the firm, Peter (known as Joe) Chamberlin (1919–78), Geoffry Powell (1920–99) and Christof Bon (1921–99), had formed a practice after Powell won the competition for the Golden Lane Estate in 1952 at the age of just 31. This estate, which would be constructed between 1952 and 1962, inaugurated the relationship with the City of London Corporation which would lead to the Barbican commission. Located right next to the Barbican, Golden Lane has a different atmosphere. Its more modest scale and use of jubilantly coloured panels and elegantly lightweight detailing contrast with the Barbican's stark robustness. Golden Lane was also meant as council housing whereas the Barbican was always conceived as being composed of 'good class' flats. Nevertheless, Golden Lane set many of the terms with which the architects conceptualised the Barbican. Especially important was the way CPB talked of the estate as being specifically *urban*: as Powell expounded, 'we regard the whole scheme as urban. We have no desire to make the project look like a garden suburb. On the contrary, *we want* to make it look urban. Therefore, you will not find large areas of grass with informal groups of trees.'[1] The ambition behind the Barbican, from the beginning, was therefore to create a piece of city that, as will be seen, celebrated *urbanity* both socially and architecturally.

CPB were not alone in this outlook, as the late 1950s and early 1960s, when the Barbican was being conceived, saw many commentators proclaiming the aesthetic and social benefits of compactly laid out development. Such ideas were not just advocated by architects and planners, but also by sociologists such as Ruth Glass, who coined the term 'gentrification', and politicians such as Labour MP Anthony Crosland. CPB were important proponents and propagandists for such arguments. They were, for example, intimately linked with the Society for the Promotion of Urban Renewal, which

Le Corbusier, Ville Radieuse, sans lieu, 1930. Le Corbusier presented his urban master plan in the 1920s and published it in 1935.

Chamberlin, Powell & Bon, Great Arthur House, Golden Lane Estate, 1952–62.

Alton Estate in Roehampton, London, photographed in 1958.

Aerial view of the Barbican Estate, photographed in 2013.

had been set up to reverse trends of decentralisation, and to affirm that cities were worth living in. This was in reaction to what was perceived as being the social sterility caused by both suburban expansion and the Garden City ideals that had been bastardized in out-of-county estates and the first generation of New Towns, such as Harlow and Stevenage. The search for urbanity also necessitated a move away from the Corbusian model of point blocks dotted among parkland, which had seen its fullest realisation in Britain at the London County Council's Alton Estate (1959), on the edge of Richmond Park. In contrast to either the Corbusian or the Garden City model of city building, the vision underpinning the Barbican was one of bringing people back to live at high density in the heart of the city, and the aesthetic ideals of formality, enclosure, views framed by buildings and compactness.

In the City of London Corporation, CPB found a commissioning body able to give them a chance to realise their vision of a high-density sociability, protected from the bustle, noise and dirt of the surrounding city, but with the convenience of work and entertainment close at hand. The gimcrack quality of so much post-war architecture was in part down to the fact of it being funded either by cash-strapped local authorities or by cynical developers. The City, in contrast, was able to put clout behind expensive detailing and full amenities. It took the dedication not just of the architects but also of many advocates within the Corporation to gain a residential scheme rather than a more profitable office development. The City had seen an extreme version of the nationwide decanting of the population away from city centres, with large-scale suburbanisation stimulated by the growth of transport networks, the planning ideals of the Garden City movement, and concerns about living conditions in densely populated slums. In the 100 years from 1851 to 1951 the population of the square mile of the city had plummeted from 130,000 inhabitants to just 5,000. The Blitz had decimated the area and intensified the dispersal of its residential population – but also created a blank canvas for grand ideas.

The first plans for the Barbican envisioned it in a style similar to that used at Golden Lane, with coloured panels and more delicate detailing. In moving towards much heavier forms and the exposed bush-hammered concrete, the Barbican was following fashion – in reaction against the lightweight style associated with the Festival of Britain of 1951 – which added flourishes of colour and whimsy to a starker Modernist idiom. Defending their use of harsher forms, CPB argued that, 'we feel strongly that other values besides refinement should be pursued, particularly clarity of form and – sometimes – robustness.'[2] This robustness relates to CPB's goal of urbanity, and echoes the architectural critic Ian Nairn's opinion that city centres shouldn't be too polite, where the danger was of the 'reduction of vitality by false genteelism'.[3] The biggest influence on the move towards a tougher aesthetic was the post-war architecture of Le Corbusier, most notably his colossal and hugely romantic *Unité d'Habitation* in Marseilles, realised in *béton brut*, ie with the concrete exposed and roughly unfinished. Although Chamberlin, Powell and Bon would have eschewed the label, it is common to see the style of the Barbican as 'brutalist'. Whether or not the Barbican is brutalist, this should not make us see it as brutal, for there is always a sombre grace, indeed a dandyism, in its finely wrought detailing. The detailing succeeds in being consistent yet varied enough not to be monotonous. It is difficult to pick out individual moments in a project of this scale. Examples of the elegantly conceived details include the way the brick floorscape curves up to meet the concrete balustrades or to make flowerbeds, the delicate pergolas over the sunken water garden marooned in the lake, and the white shell-like barrel vaults crowning each of the slab blocks.

One of the most appealing things about the Barbican is how it was never meant to be just a housing estate, but a full community based around cosmopolitan and cultured pursuits. The Barbican reflects a vision of the good life in affluent 1950s Britain. Some of the features the architects proposed to include – such as a shopping centre or the

Bush-hammered concrete, Frobisher Crescent, Barbican.

Chimneys from the electricity substation next to Frobisher Crescent and Cromwell Tower.

A sketch showing
St Giles' Cripplegate
church and illustrating
CPB's first proposal for
the Barbican, 1955.

placing of reconstructed historic London buildings such as
Sir Christopher Wren's Temple Bar Gate or James Bunstone
Bunnings's Coal Exchange at points throughout the site –
never came to fruition. It nevertheless incorporates a wealth
of amenities: not just the arts centre, but gardens with a range
of different characters, restaurants and cafes, as well as the
Guildhall School of Music and Drama and the City of London
School for Girls.

The Barbican grew out of a moment in which there
was a presumption that ever-increasing economic growth
would provide the basis for uninterrupted social progress,
bringing with it an 'abundance of goods and gadgets, of
cars and new buildings – in an apparently mounting flow
of consumption.'[4] Planners and architects of the period
attempted to channel this growth towards a vision of a better
society. The Barbican echoes the political discourse of its
time, which saw the abundance of the affluent society as
necessitating a renewed focus on issues of culture, recreation
and the physical environment. As a 1959 Labour Party policy
document put it, 'the emphasis will increasingly be not on
jobs for all but leisure for all – leisure *and how to use it.*'[5]
The Barbican was created for those who had benefited
from this affluence and the expanded horizons that
it stimulated; people who, as the architects described
them, were 'young professionals, likely to have a taste for
Mediterranean holidays, French food and Scandinavian
design.'[6] In such a sentence the architects could have been
describing themselves.

The post-war growth of traffic was a major concern of
the period, with wide-ranging implications for planning and
architectural thought. The number of licensed motor vehicles
in Britain had doubled from 4.5 million to 9 million between
1950 and 1960, and was correctly predicted to carry on
rising. The 'motorcar revolution' was seen to invalidate
traditional layouts of cities – the structure of a building next
to a pavement next to a road – on which London with its
system of streets and squares had been based for centuries.

Cars made old cities impracticable; as a 1960 policy document put it:

> [...] what has finally shattered the old scene, both in small towns and large ones, during the past generation or two has been the arrival of the universal motor-car – with its threat of delay, distraction and death. The same street pattern still exists but it is now filled with a tangle of buses, taxis, delivery vans, private cars, cycles and pedestrians, both stationary and moving (or at least wishing to), delaying, harassing, injuring and even killing each other.[7]

Segregation of vehicles and pedestrians seemed to offer a panacea to these concerns. There were two ways to achieve such segregation. The first was through a 'pedestrian precinct', which relegated traffic to the perimeter of a site. Pedestrian precincts were a major feature of the planning vocabulary of the 1950s, most visible in the central shopping areas in the first generation of New Towns, but also influential on housing layouts, including Golden Lane.

The Barbican was representative of a new, more radical, way to achieve segregation, in that it placed all the living functions of a city on a 'deck' or 'podium' above traffic, garages and servicing. The Barbican creates a new pedestrian level, generally around six metres above ground, although it is made to feel much higher as areas such as the gardens and lake are sunk down to several meters below ground level. It was a complex engineering feat, carried out in consultation with Ove Arup. The estate was originally meant to be part of a much larger system of upper-level walkways and decks, the strangely named 'pedway', which was going to stretch throughout London, although only intermittent parts were ever completed. The concept of multi-level planning was in the air when the Barbican was conceived. It was promoted by, among others, Alison and Peter Smithson in their Berlin Hauptstadt competition (1957), Colin Buchanan in *Traffic in Towns* (1963), and in the schemes for the town centres of

The elevated walkway, Gilbert Bridge, Barbican. The 'yellow line' was introduced in the late 1970s to the walkways around the estate as a means of facilitating navigation to the Barbican Centre.

One of the residents' gardens of the Barbican, seen from the deck.

Hook and Cumbernauld New Towns, and in new Universities such as Denys Lasdun's University of East Anglia and the Architect's Co-Partnership's University of Essex (as well as CPB's own Leeds campus). The Barbican, however, is by far the most significant realisation of such ideas in Britain. It embodies both the advantages and disadvantages of upper-level segregation. In relegating traffic, a space is created where, as CPB put it themselves, 'people will be able to move about freely enjoying constantly changing perspectives.'[8] On the other hand, the Barbican connects poorly with the rest of the city, it does not provide easily navigable through routes apart from the underground road tunnel, and it is inward looking.

The way CPB presented this seemingly ultramodern idea of upper-level decks was devoid of futurism. Instead they stressed the way that it was located in a tradition of London building, as they put it:

> The principle of a podium with terraces above is, of course, not new and can be seen today in Carlton House Terrace. The old Adelphi was a complex example of the application of this principle of separating traffic on different levels.[9]

The reference to Sir William Chambers's Carlton House Terrace (1827–32) and to Robert Adam's Adelphi (1768–72), may strike a reader as odd when considering what a radical and seemingly Modernist idea CPB were proposing. However, it is indicative of an important feature of CPB's approach: the merging of radical forms and historical suggestions. The plans for the Barbican are replete with references to traditional London typologies. Alongside the Modernist housing typologies of point blocks and slabs raised on pilotis, the Barbican attempts to reintroduce into this radical scheme many spaces that are evocative of London's *genius loci* (spirit of the place). London's garden squares, mews housing, crescents, Albany in Piccadilly, and the Inns of Court were all cited. The belief that planning a city on a deck would allow architects to reinvest in traditional forms, but in a way free from the horrors of traffic, was common at the time. The Barbican realises the ambition expressed in Buchanan's influential 1963 manual *Traffic in Towns*:

> This deck would, in effect, comprise a new ground level, and upon it the buildings would rise in a pattern related to but not dictated by the traffic below. On the deck it would be possible to re-create, in an even better form, the things that have delighted man for generations in towns – the snug, the close, varied atmosphere, the narrow alleys, the contrasting open squares, the effects of light and shade, the fountains and the sculpture.[10]

The various elements that make up the Barbican, both high Modernist and historically suggestive, are merged together in a way which displays the influence of the post-war Townscape movement, centred on *The Architectural Review*, which advocated bringing the ideas of the 18th-century Picturesque to bear on modern development, so as to overcome the monotony of new forms of building and orthogonal layouts. It is notable that one of the key Townscape propagandists, Gordon Cullen, drew the early perspectives for CPB. The Barbican's picturesque sensibility is so theatrical and exuberant that it has led many to see it in a tradition stretching back to the English Baroque architect Sir John Vanbrugh. That the Barbican is simultaneously reminiscent of a futurist Metropolis and a *béton brut* Blenheim Palace is remarkable and characteristic. It is a project of merging contradictions: it embraces modern technology and high culture, is monolithic and intricate, Modernist and historically suggestive, domestic yet grand, urban yet secluded. It is a bravura piece of place-making, worthy of comparison with examples from any period.

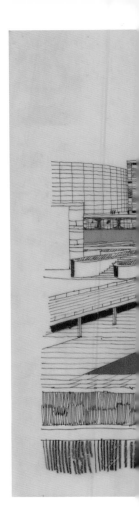

1956

Gordon Cullen's
visualisation of the
Barbican scheme
proposed by CPB
in 1956 showing an
early pyramid-shaped
conservatory.

'The Barbican is what all ambitious housing projects of half a century ought to have been. The fact that it is an atypical success says less about the quality of its architecture than the neglect and indifference that other projects suffered. The Barbican is like a well-made car – a Bristol, say – which has been constantly serviced and cherished. Most estates were like Triumph Dolomites which were never maintained. It is this matter of upkeep that is more pertinent than the classist argument that high-rise works only for the bourgeoisie but baffles blue-collars. That is snobbery which is manifestly untrue. The Barbican, too, could have achieved sink estate status had it not been properly guarded. As it is, it remains one of the joys of London, sculptural, awe-inspiring and symptomatic of an optimism that has dissipated. The extent to which it is currently revered suggests that it takes several decades for popular thought to catch up with architectural thought. Maybe we should be less hasty about ridding ourselves of what dullards reckon to be monstrosities and carbuncles.'

Jonathan Meades

Barbican before Barbican

On the west side of the Red crosse, is a streete called the
Barbican, because sometime there stoode on the North
side thereof, a Burgh-Kening or Watch Tower of the Cittie
called in some language a Barbican.

John Stow, *A Survey of London*, 1603

Today, the Barbican is a residential estate, an arts centre and
a Tube stop, but beneath its famous concrete towers, concert
hall and theatre, lies a rich history reaching back almost
2,000 years. When the Elizabethan historian John Stow
wrote his survey of London, the Barbican was a street, although
he noted that its name went back to earlier times, when a
watchtower – a barbican – overlooked the countryside beyond
the walls of London. Before that, in AD 200 the Romans had
built a defensive wall around their settlement Londinium which
continued to be maintained until the 17th century. Today, ruins
still survive, as do the names of the gates, for example Ludgate,
Aldgate and Aldersgate. Cripplegate, on the north side
of the wall, marked the boundary between the City, known
as Cripplegate-Within, and the moorland suburbs, known
as Cripplegate-Without. The history of Cripplegate-Without
before the 16th century is largely a matter of conjecture, but
in 1090 Alfune, Bishop of London, founded the church of
St Giles' without Cripplegate, which has since undergone
many reconstructions but is still in use.

A map of the area dating from the mid-16th century shows
tightly packed gabled houses within the city walls and more
sparsely built land beyond Cripplegate in the parish of St Giles
Cripplegate with fields and windmills in the distance. At the
end of the 16th century, Cripplegate-Without was inhabited by

The remains of a
bastion of the Roman
city wall and the church
of St Giles' Cripplegate.

more than 4,000 people. Entertainment for the growing population was provided by Philip Henslowe's acting company, the Admiral's Men, which performed at the Fortune Theatre which opened in 1600 between Golden Lane and Whitecross Street. Residents included William Shakespeare and later, the author of *Paradise Lost*, John Milton. The 1660s was marked by two disasters: the Great Plague of London in 1665, which killed almost 8,000 people in St Giles' parish, and the Great Fire in 1666, which ravaged the City of London, although most of Cripplegate-Without survived unscathed. Following these events the area declined and became increasingly overcrowded as the wealthier households moved away and the large properties were demolished to be replaced by smaller homes. However, by the 1750s new businesses revitalised Cripplegate, including Samuel Whitbread's brewery in Chiswell Street and George Seddon's furniture emporium, which both became famous. By then, it was also home to the trade-halls of barbers, haberdashers, wax chandlers, brewers and glovers.[1]

The 19th century heralded major transformations for the Barbican area. Large portions of land, which had previously been occupied by private houses, were given over to rail development and warehouses, leading to a dramatic drop in the resident population while over 20,000 commuted daily, in a trend that has since increased. In 1897, a devastating fire broke out in an ostrich-feather warehouse and spread swiftly from textile warehouses to small businesses. The damage was soon repaired, and photographs taken at the beginning of the 20th century reveal streets bustling with clerks, tradesmen and horse-drawn carts.

The entire ward of Cripplegate was destroyed, however, in a single night of the Blitz. On 29 December 1940, a deluge of incendiary bombs fell over the City, particularly between Moorgate and Aldersgate. Once again, fire swept through the area and by the end of the war, little remained save for the outer shell of St Giles' Cripplegate and the Fire Station on Red Cross Street.

Barbican from the end of Red Cross Street and Golden Lane looking west, 1921.

The destruction caused by the Blitz was recorded by City of London Police Constables Arthur Cross and Fred Tibbs. The photographs show bomb damage at Whitecross Street and St Giles' Cripplegate church, 1940.

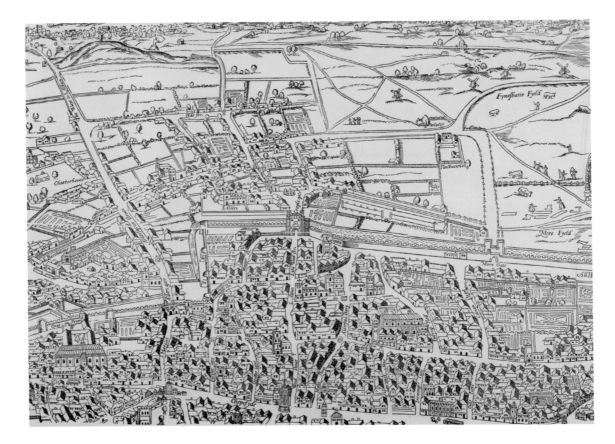

Detail from the
'Agas' map of London,
c 1560, showing
the Barbican area
beyond Cripplegate.

The Barbican site
when construction
began, 1963.

'Why shouldn't I love the Barbican? I'm in Heaven at a concert or play. Going is a privilege, a treat, an occasion. I love the space; outside, getting there is a mini adventure of anticipation; and inside, during intervals the open space is cosy because there is so much going on and you can see everyone and you feel you're protected in this large complex by the pleasure of it all.'

Vivienne Westwood

Chamberlin, Powell & Bon

In 1952, a young architect named Geoffry Powell won a competition to build a housing estate on land north of what was later to become the Barbican. The Golden Lane Estate was instigated by the City of London Corporation to bring residents back into the area and to provide accommodation for City workers. Powell was then teaching at the Department of Architecture of Kingston School of Art where he had met fellow-architects Peter (known as Joe) Chamberlin and Christof Bon. They had strategically decided to each submit a design to the competition on the understanding that if one of them won, they would form a practice. Golden Lane Estate thus launched Chamberlin, Powell & Bon (CPB). This was a major commission by any standard, and even more so for young architects who had until then built very little. Golden Lane also proved a pivotal project for the architects as they established a relationship with the Corporation, which eventually appointed them to design and build the Barbican.

The practice brought together three very different, but each extraordinarily talented, architects. Joe Chamberlin (1919–78) was the practice's natural leader and played a key role managing the sometimes fraught relationship with the Corporation. Born in London, he had studied Philosophy, Politics and Economics at Pembroke College in Oxford in the late 1930s and humorously commented later that the course, 'although pompous sounding was nevertheless intriguing.'[1] As a committed pacifist, Chamberlin was a conscientious objector during the war and worked instead as a farm labourer and then in the civil defence for the Air Raids Precautions in London.[2] In 1940, he married Jean Bingham, whose enthusiasm and strong character meant she became a pillar of the practice.

Joe Chamberlin and
Jean Bingham with
friends at the University
of Oxford, late 1930s.

Geoffry Powell at
Avenue Studios,
London, 1956.

Chamberlin joined Kingston School of Architecture in 1941.
He had sent his wife to enquire about a woodworking course
and 'by a series of accidents, she signed him up for a course in
architecture [...] and because he became intensely absorbed
in [the] subject, eventually "qualified".'[3]

Christof Bon (1921–99) was born in St Gallen in Switzerland,
where his father and uncle owned the luxurious Suvretta House
hotel in St Moritz. He qualified as an architect at the Swiss
Federal Institute of Technology in Zurich before coming to
England in 1946 to assist William Holford who was then
working on the Corporation's reconstruction plan for London.
Bon then joined the pioneering Modernist architectural firm
BBPR (Banfi, Belgiojoso, Peressutti and Rogers) in Milan,
and in 1948 returned to England to teach at Kingston School
of Architecture, where he met Chamberlin and Powell. For
practical reasons, he soon became Jean and Joe Chamberlin's
lodger. In fact, the trio found such living arrangements so
suitable that Bon never left, and they continued to live and
work together.

Born in India to a military family, Geoffry Powell (1920–99)
was destined for an army career until a serious illness left him
unfit for service. He studied at the Architectural Association in
London initially because, as he later wittily explained, 'it seemed
an easy option' but soon 'discovered what it was about, partly
through reading Corb [Le Corbusier] and it became the most
important thing in my life.'[4] Powell became an assistant to
Frederick Gibberd in 1944 and to Brian O'Rorke in 1946,
before joining the staff at Kingston School of Architecture in
1949.[5] Powell's wide-ranging interests included horticulture
and landscape gardening as well as travelling and archaeology

- the latter two passions are reflected in his watercolours of architecture and ancient ruins. His paintings reveal an architect's appreciation for monumentality, a quality also to be found in the work of his favourite architect, the creator of Blenheim Palace: Sir John Vanbrugh.

Although the Barbican was a colossal project and dominated the practice for almost 30 years (1955–82), they also produced and realised distinctive and imaginative designs for, among others, Cooper Taber Co., a seed factory at Witham, Essex (1954–6); Bousefield Primary School, London (1953–6); New Hall, now Murray Edwards College, Cambridge (1958–66); Birmingham University Physical Education Centre (1959–66); Vanbrugh Park housing in Greenwich, London (1959–65); and Leeds University Development (1960–78). After Chamberlin's early death in 1978, the partnership continued and was restructured in 1985 to become Chamberlin, Powell, Bon and Woods, with Frank Woods, who had joined the firm in 1959, becoming a partner. In 1987 the firm was merged with the larger practice Austin-Smith:Lord.

Chamberlin, Powell and Bon shared a sense of humour and liberal values, believing that architecture was for the greater good. As a former partner of CPB (Barbican), John Honer, remembers:

> The cement that held the partnership together for so long was a vision of the city that exists not just in support of commercial interests but also as a civilised place in which to live and work. This was manifest not only in the design of the buildings themselves, but also in the relationship between the internal and external spaces, and in the provision of properly landscaped areas.[6]

Geoffry Powell's photographs of Le Corbusier's Unité d'Habitation, Marseilles, which he visited while it was under construction between 1947 and 1952.

Christof Bon on the right and colleagues at the CPB practice in Lamont Road Passage, London, 1970s.

FROM LEFT Geoffry Powell, Christof Bon and Joe Chamberlin standing outside Avenue Studios, off Fulham Road, London. (*The Architects' Journal*, 15 Jan 1953).

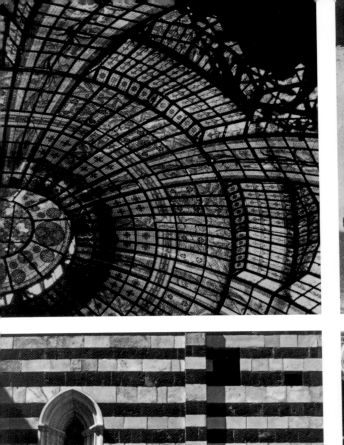

OPPOSITE All three
partners were keen
photographers, and
each year they selected
one of their photographs
to reproduce on
the firm's Christmas
and New Year card.
(CLOCKWISE FROM TOP LEFT
Paris; Ano Mera, Island
of Mykonos; Venice and
unidentified place).

This watercolour by
Geoffry Powell reveals
his appreciation of
bold contrasts of light
and shadow, and of
robust architecture.

Bousefield Primary
School, London, 1953–6.

New Hall (now Murray
Edwards College),
Cambridge, 1958–66.

Leeds University
Development, 1960–78.

'The image of the Barbican is memorable for its permanence. At a distance its three distinctive towers with their telltale silhouette, sharpened by their triangular plan forms, play against each other like the stand of a petrified forest. Within, in contrast, is the unexpected softness of its gardens, the sound of its fountains and cascade, and the terraces spilling out southwards from the plenitude of its creative and cultural offerings. We can too easily take for granted the quality and care with which it was made, and through this it will serve many generations to come, absorbing changes with ease. The ambition now must be to activate its girth and to connect its inner world at street level to the growing city around it.'

Eric Parry

The Architects' Proposals

In the aftermath of the Blitz, the City of London Corporation acquired much of the ruined land of the Barbican site with the intention of re-establishing it as a commercial district. However, its priorities changed in 1953 with discussions about a new law proposing that the power of an authority depend on the size of its resident electorate. Although thousands flocked daily to the City, over the preceding century it had witnessed a dramatic fall in its population, and in 1951 only 48 people lived in the ward of Cripplegate.[1] The Corporation therefore changed its policy to one that would actively bolster the electorate and began encouraging proposals that allowed for at least some residential accommodation in the Barbican area.

Although fierce opposition to a residential scheme persisted among members of the Corporation who favoured a more lucrative office development, a group championed the idea of building housing in the City. It included Eric Wilkins, Chairman of the Public Health Committee of the Corporation, who was a supporter of the Golden Lane Estate then being built to a design by Chamberlin, Powell & Bon (CPB). Wilkins recommended that the Corporation employ CPB as consultant architects for the Barbican residential development, and continued to be a key advocate of the scheme.[2] CPB began work on the Barbican in the mid-1950s, and the arts centre – the final part of the development – was inaugurated in 1982. Between 1955 and 1959, the partners and the numerous architects of their thriving practice produced three different schemes, each time responding to the Corporation's changing requirements, in which they teased out the Barbican's layout, function and character before the residential components of the 1959 scheme were approved for construction.

In their 1955 preliminary report for a residential estate on the site of the Barbican, CPB proposed a network of four-storey residential blocks arranged around tree-planted courtyards, with taller blocks of flats on the edges of the estate. The architects suggested building to a high density (300 persons to the acre) in order that the high cost of the land might be offset by the rent from a large number of tenants, and so make the scheme financially viable for the Corporation. They also paid close attention to public open spaces and turned the church of St Giles' Cripplegate into the focal point of the pedestrian estate, surrounding the church square with shops, restaurants, pubs and new premises for the Guildhall School of Music and Drama. This scheme also included an exhibition hall and sports facilities for the benefit of the residents.

However, the Corporation rejected this scheme on the grounds that the density of population was too high and that there was insufficient open space. The Corporation therefore added more land to the north and also asked the architects to include two further schools in the scheme: the City of London School and the City of London School for Girls. In the centre of their revised scheme, CPB grouped together the three schools (including the Guildhall School) so that the theatre, concert hall and assembly halls could serve as a cultural centre for the residents when they were not used by the schools. The 1956 scheme contained many of the elements that featured in the final plans for the Barbican: the three residential towers, the terrace blocks and a cultural hub, which eventually developed into the Barbican Centre. During these years, there was no certainty that CPB's proposals would be adopted. Schemes including commercial developments continued to be discussed until 1957 when the Corporation accepted as a matter of policy the recommendation from the Minister of Housing and Local Government, Duncan Sandys, that the Barbican be developed as 'a genuine residential neighbourhood, incorporating schools, shops, open spaces and amenities, even if this means foregoing a more remunerative return on the land.'[3]

In 1959, CPB presented a revised scheme which again took into account revisions to the Corporation's requirements. Significantly, the architects were asked to develop a network of elevated walkways, segregating pedestrians from vehicles, which were to connect with similar walkways within an area of office developments then under construction to the south of the Barbican. The Corporation also required the architects to provide open spaces and gardens as well as parking space, and to consider integrating the Victorian-era cast-iron structure of the Coal Exchange, which was then threatened with demolition. While the Coal Exchange was to form a central atrium to the Guildhall School of Music and Drama, the architects expanded the arts centre so that it included a theatre, art gallery and lending library. This scheme was approved for construction and, in May 1960, CPB were finally appointed architects to the Barbican. The building began in September 1963.[4]

A map of the Barbican Estate site showing the pre-Blitz street layout in CPB's 1959 report about the redevelopment of the Barbican.

─ ●●● ─	City Boundary
─ ─ ─ ─	Comprehensive Redevelopment
▬▬▬▬	Boundaries of the Site in the terms of Reference

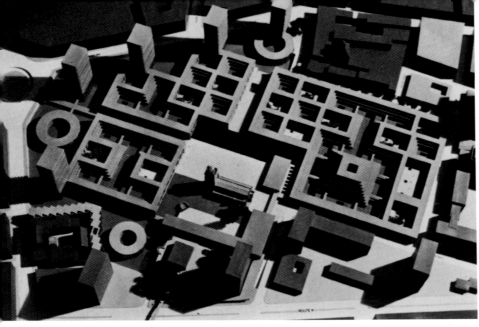

Model of CPB's 1955 Barbican proposal. The architects explained they had aimed at 'the secluded, cloistered atmosphere characteristic of Albany and the Inns of Court.'

Model of CPB's 1956 Barbican proposal. In this scheme they introduced the idea of the three residential towers, the terrace blocks wrapping around gardens and the crescent-shaped building, all of which became key features of the Barbican as it was built.

FROM LEFT Powell, Bon and Chamberlin present their model for the Barbican redevelopment, 1956.

Model of CPB's 1959 proposal, which was approved for construction and later modified.

Visualisation of the
1956 scheme.

Gordon Cullen, view looking west under the bridge connecting The Postern and Andrewes House.

Gordon Cullen, view looking south-west at podium level underneath Gilbert House.

Norah Glover drew
a series of sketches
of the Barbican before
it was built to visualise
the lively and utopian
quarter imagined
by CPB.

Norah Glover,
visualisation of the
1959 scheme looking
towards the City of
London School for Girls.

Norah Glover,
two visualisations
of the residential
terrace blocks.

Visualisation
of the Barbican
residential blocks.

LEFT Shakespeare Tower
under construction, 1972.

OPPOSITE Barbican Estate
under construction, 1969.

'For most, brutalism is a miserable danger zone of concrete car park or pee stained walkways on a wind swept council estate, but the Barbican reminds us of how different it could all have been.

The generosity of materiality, the monumental public spaces, the integration of living spaces, culture and public interaction is a long misunderstood, due to be re-assessed exemplar of city regeneration and community building – funded by the public purse for the common good.'

Tom Dixon

Lifestyle

Largely planned in the mid-to-late 1950s, the Barbican is a product of the post-war and post-austerity sense of optimism and faith in modern developments. Unlike the nearby Golden Lane Estate, also designed by Chamberlin, Powell & Bon (CPB), the Barbican's residential blocks were never intended as social housing. Instead these luxurious flats, built between 1964 and 1975, were aimed at a range of affluent and middle-class City tenants who could afford the high rents demanded by the City of London Corporation and who aspired to a new and modern lifestyle.

The Barbican's famous towers and barrel-roofed terrace blocks include over 2,000 flats in a vast variety of layouts ranging from studios to four-bedroom flats, with a few five-bedroom houses. In these urban homes, CPB defined modern luxury in a high-density estate: they adopted the latest and most functional conveniences, created dramatic vistas, used limited space to its best advantage and designed many of the fittings specifically, doing away with traditional ornamentation and endowing the Barbican with its characteristic sophisticated style. As the architects explained in their 1959 report on the redevelopment of the Barbican:

> Architecturally, our aim has been to design an overall layout which will become an environment highly desirable to live in. To this end we have given great attention both to the design of the individual buildings and of the space between them.[1]

At the time they were designed, the Barbican flats were extremely modern – when most older English homes still relied on open fireplaces, the Barbican offered electric

A section of a Garchey waste-disposal unit fitted to a sink.

TWYFORDS hand rinse basins

IN VITREOUS CHINA

Twyford advert for the Barbican hand-rinse basin, 1960s.

underfloor heating. The architects also anticipated the growth of consumer goods such as refrigerators and cars and conceived the blocks so that lifts connected the flats to underground parking, with the idea that most households would eventually own a car. Streamlined fully fitted kitchens were equipped with space-saving storage and stainless steel surfaces into which were set the cooking hobs and sinks. One of the two sinks in each kitchen was equipped with a Garchey waste-disposal system which flushed refuse down the drain to collection chambers. Although this system may now seem eccentric and unhygienic, it was in use in other developments and the architects favoured it because it was quieter than chutes and cheaper than paying staff to collect waste.

Much of the style of the Barbican flats is owed to the architects' lavish attention to fittings such as door handles and switches, each of which was designed specifically for the Barbican. For instance, the exceptionally shallow hand-rinse basins in the lavatories were an ingenious response to the new recommendation that every separate toilet have a basin. Rather than change the layout of the flat to accommodate a standard basin, Chamberlin, Powell & Bon created a radically new one which has become an icon of 1960s design.

The environment surrounding the residential blocks was crucial to the scheme, for the architects understood that wealthy tenants would expect the estate to offer not only refined detailing inside the flats but also a pleasant lifestyle. One of the architects' greatest concerns was therefore to limit noise levels. The railway linking Moorgate to Barbican stations was covered and the tracks were suspended to reduce vibrations and noise, while Beech Street, which would otherwise have crossed through the estate, was covered with a walkway. The network of elevated walkways allowed the architects to create 'a pedestrian oasis free from traffic.'[2]

Landscaping, including the lush gardens and the lake, played an essential role, acting as a foil to the grandiose architecture. In a similar way to traditional London squares, the gardens were reserved to residents and added to the appeal of the estate and to its sense of privacy in the middle of the busy City. As well as gardens and attractive vistas, the estate was intended to provide the residents with a multitude of other amenities including shops, restaurants and pubs, and an arts centre which gradually expanded in the successive schemes of the development.

Pamphlet promoting
Cromwell Tower flats,
early 1970s.

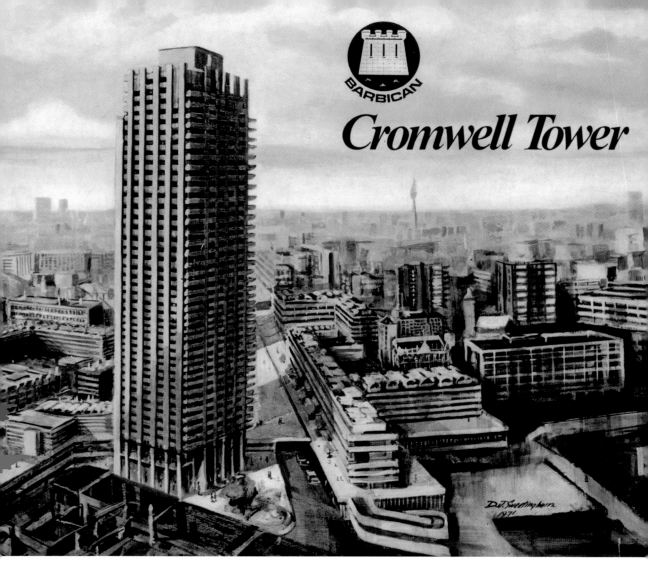

BARBICAN

Cromwell Tower

Living Room

Sliding partitions are provided in flat types B & C to obtain maximum flexibility of use. Large side sliding picture windows afford extension of room on to spacious balcony.

Sales pamphlet showing the interior of Cromwell Tower, early 1970s.

Entrance Foyer

Spacious entrance foyer/lounge with Porter in attendance 24 hours per day. Entryphone service to each flat.

Mountjoy House

Living Room
in typical flat

The living and dining
area in a flat in Speed
House, which was
the first block to be
completed, in 1968.

The kitchen and
dining area in one of
the flats, 1970. Leaflets
advertised the luxury
kitchens fully fitted with
built-in refrigerators
and split-level cookers,
mechanical ventilation,
stainless-steel double
sinks and Garchey
refuse-disposal units.

Double height area in a duplex flat in Gilbert House, photographed in 2009.

Interior details of a
duplex flat in Gilbert
House, photographed
in 2009.

Delivery hatches,
Gilbert House flat,
photographed in 2013.
Each flat was provided
with tradesmen's
delivery hatches built
into the entrance door.

Living room area,
Brandon Mews,
photographed
in 2013.

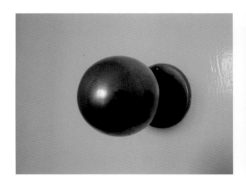

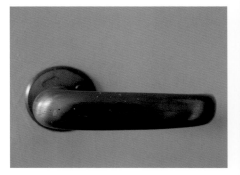

Fittings designed
for the Barbican,
Cromwell Tower.

Entryphone system
in Lauderdale Tower,
mirroring the building's
silhouette.

OPPOSITE Lift lobby in
Barbican Tower. In
their 1959 report, CPB
explained: 'The finishes
to the public parts –
halls, internal access
ways and stairs – are of
particular importance
since they set a standard
and play a large
part in establishing
the character of the
residential buildings.'

'When I was a young assistant director at the Royal Shakespeare Theatre in Stratford-upon-Avon in 1967, one of our most pleasurable diversions was to go into what was called 'The Associates' Room' and to gloat over the large-scale model of the glorious futuristic theatre that was, one day in the distant future, destined to be the new London home of the Royal Shakespeare Company at the Barbican. Eventually I had the privilege of enjoying this delightful performance space, with its ample legroom and moderate maximum distance from the stage for even the furthest spectator. Since that time the Barbican Centre has become a central feature of one's cultural life — theatrical, cinematic, musical and visual — and you can even avail yourself of a decent hot dinner there. Even what was at one time the ordeal of finding one's way has been replaced by the simple satisfaction of following the yellow brick road! And now, as Chairman of the London Film School, I'm delighted to have become directly involved with the Barbican, as we plan the School's intended move into the Centre in the not-too-distant future. It is going to be very exciting.'

Mike Leigh

Barbican Centre

When it was opened in 1982, the Barbican Centre was far removed from the cultural centre Chamberlin, Powell & Bon (CPB) had envisioned for the benefit of the estate's residents in their 1956 proposal. It had grown into the largest multi-arts centre in Europe, consisting of the Guildhall School of Music and Drama, a concert hall, a theatre, an art gallery, cinemas, a public lending library, catering facilities, foyers and car-parking facilities.

Although the 1959 scheme had been approved, it continued changing even as it was being built: the road cutting across the site was abandoned, as was the plan to re-erect the Coal Exchange. Instead, the City of London Corporation instructed CPB to redesign the Guildhall School and the arts centre as independent from one another so that the theatre and concert hall could be used throughout the year by professional companies. By 1964, the theatre, concert hall and library each required more space. The architects were therefore faced with the challenge of fitting a growing arts centre into a space restricted by housing under construction. Because building the arts centre above ground would have obstructed the views of some of the flats, CPB decided to fit the majority of the centre below the elevated walkway level, known as the 'podium'. When the architects presented their new design for the arts centre in a report in 1968, they compared it to a ship, explaining that 'in many ways the Arts Centre has [...] much in common with the hull of a large ship in which much is contained below the water [...].'[1]

The Corporation invited the Royal Shakespeare Company (RSC) and the London Symphony Orchestra (LSO) to take up a permanent residency at the centre, so CPB designed the

Barbican Centre
foyer showing Hadrian
seating by Robin
Day and sculpture by
Michael Santry, c 1980.

theatre and the concert hall to the companies' specifications. In the 1,200 seat theatre auditorium, the architects devised an ingenious structure of cantilevered seats which relied on the properties of pre-stressed concrete to hang the balconies forward instead of receding them as in traditional theatres. This was partly a solution to the limited space, but it was essentially a way of bringing the audience closer to the stage. Beneath the theatre is a small auditorium which was designed as the RSC's rehearsal theatre. It became known as The Pit after workmen digging out the space discovered a medieval grave. To store the RSC's large number of stage sets for its Shakespearean repertory, the architects suggested constructing a tall fly tower that rose above the podium level and proposed wrapping a conservatory around it to conceal its imposing concrete structure, while adding an attractive feature.

The concert hall, accommodating an audience of 2,000, was built for the LSO for symphonic music. However, in a bid to make the arts centre financially viable, the Corporation also required that it be a flexible space that could be used for conferences. The acoustics of the hall were one of the essential preoccupations of the architects who were concerned the quality of sound would be affected by the limited space. Following advice from specialist consultants, 1,700 Perspex spheres were initially hung to the roof as it was thought they would improve the quality of the sound. After the centre's inauguration, the acoustics continued to be improved, and between 2000 and 2001 Caruso St John Architects and US acoustics design firm Kirkegaard Associates devised a system of reflectors that improved the sound in the hall.

The art gallery and library were conceived together around a central well which connected both venues. All of the spaces were linked by grand staircases that were intended to allow visitors to move freely between them. CPB suggested that the roof of the hall, a semi-circular terrace delineated by Frobisher Crescent, could be used by the neighbouring art gallery as a sculpture court or as an outdoor concert space and would contribute to creating a vibrant and urban atmosphere in the residential estate. Shops and cafes were envisaged for the semi-circular walkway below.

The unity of the vast scheme was maintained by a common language running through the housing estate and the arts centre, including the tooling of the concrete structural elements, which gives it its characteristic rough concrete finish, the massive 'boat edge' balustrades which mark the podium level, and the brass finishings. CPB embraced the Corporation's requirement for elevated walkways and intended visitors to access the Centre from the podium level or via the grand *porte cochère* below street level, if arriving by car. However, contrary to the Corporation's hopes, the pedestrian raised network did not spread across the City, leaving the Barbican Centre arguably difficult to access. In the early 1990s, Theo Crosby of the design practice Pentagram, and artist Polly Hope made some cosmetic changes which were widely considered unsuccessful, before the architects of Allford Hall Monaghan Morris (AHMM) were tasked with improving the circulation in the Centre between 2002 and 2006. Crucially, they created a street-level entrance on Silk Street and a bridge across the foyer to the lakeside which has made the arts centre more cohesive.

In the foyer of the Barbican Centre, *Disruption: A Fashion Performance*, Barbican Lates, 2011.

The conservatory.

The Guildhall School of Music and Drama, with Gilbert House across the lake and Cromwell Tower in the background.

ABOVE Trisha Brown's *Walking on the Wall*, first performed in 1971 and restaged at Barbican Art Gallery as part of the exhibition *Laurie Anderson, Trisha Brown, Gordon Matta-Clark: Pioneers of the Downtown Scene, New York 1970s*, 2011.

RIGHT Staircase approach to the Art Gallery and Sculpture Court from the podium on the west side of the Barbican Centre. The photograph shows one of the distinctive white tiled cantilevers, and two ventilation and service shafts, with Frobisher Crescent in the background. It is thought that CPB intended this to be an important external entrance to the gallery.

Barbican Theatre auditorium. By eliminating all gangways and placing doors at the end of each row for access, the architects used the space to its best advantage and increased the number of well-placed seats.

Looking down to the stage from the fly tower, Barbican Theatre.

LEFT Barbican Hall hung with the Perspex spheres, 1981.

RIGHT Norah Glover's visualisation of the Barbican Hall, 1968.

Seating designed by Robin Day for the Barbican Hall.

Notes

Concrete City

1 Geoffry Powell, 'Golden Lane Housing Scheme', *AA Journal* (Apr 1957), pp. 214–23, p. 216.
2 'The Architects Reply', *The Architects' Journal* (27 Jun 1957), pp. 947–8.
3 Ian Nairn, *Outrage* (London, 1955), p. 363.
4 Ruth Glass, *London Aspects of Change* (London, 1964), p. xiv.
5 Labour Party, *Leisure for Living* (London, 1959).
6 http://news.bbc.co.uk/onthisday/hi/dates/stories/january/24/newsid_3390000/3390271.stm
7 *Change and Challenge: Next Steps in Town and Country Planning* (London, 1962), p. 14.
8 Chamberlin, Powell & Bon, *Barbican Redevelopment 1959: Report to the Court of Common Council of the Corporation of the City of London on Residential Redevelopment within the Barbican Area* (London, 1959), Proposal, p. 1.
9 Ibid, p. 5.
10 Colin Buchanan, *Traffic in Towns* (London, 1963), p. 46.

Barbican Before Barbican

1 John Noorthouck, *A New History of London: Including Westminster and Southwark* (London, 1773).

Chamberlin, Powell & Bon

1 'Chamberlin, Powell & Bon', *The Architects' Journal*, (15 Jan 1953), p. 72.
2 Elain Harwood, *Chamberlin, Powell & Bon* (London, 2012), p. 12.
3 'Chamberlin, Powell & Bon', *The Architects' Journal*, (15 Jan 1953), p.72.
4 Geoffry Powell quoted in Kenneth Powell, 'People Pioneering Urbanism', *The Architects' Journal* (3 Mar 1999), pp. 24-5, p. 25.
5 Elain Harwood, *Chamberlin, Powell & Bon* (London, 2012), p. 11.
6 John Honer, 'Golden Lane Housing', public talk (27 Nov 2006).

The Architects' Proposals

1 Chamberlin, Powell & Bon, *Barbican Redevelopment 1959* (London, 1959), Introduction, p. 1.
2 David Heathcote. *Barbican: Penthouse Over the City* (London, 2004), p. 66.

3 Letter quoted in *Barbican* (London, 1971), p. 2
4 Elain Harwood, *Chamberlin, Powell & Bon* (London, 2012), p. 120.

Lifestyle

1 Chamberlin, Powell & Bon, *Barbican Redevelopment 1959* (London, 1959), p. 56.
2 Ibid, p. 7.

Barbican Centre

1 Chamberlin, Powell & Bon, *Barbican Arts Centre, 1968: Report to the Court of Common Council of the Corporation of the City of London on the Arts Centre within the Barbican Area* (London, 1968), Technical Considerations, paragraph 1.

Select Bibliography

Barbican (London, 1971).

Nicholas Bullock, *Building the Post-War World Modern Architecture and Reconstruction in Britain* (London, 2002).

Chamberlin, Powell & Bon, *Barbican Redevelopment 1959: Report to the Court of Common Council of the Corporation of the City of London on Residential Redevelopment within the Barbican Area* (London, 1959).

Chamberlin, Powell & Bon, *Barbican Arts Centre 1968: Report to the Court of Common Council of the Corporation of the City of London on the Arts Centre within the Barbican area* (London, 1968).

Jennifer Clarke, *The Barbican: Sitting on History,* (London, 1990).

Alexander Clement, *Brutalism: Post-war British Architecture,* (Ramsbury, 2011).

Lionel Esher, *The Broken Wave, The Rebuilding of England,* (London, 1981).

John R. Gold, *The Practice of Modernism: Modern Architects and Urban Transformation 1954-1972,* (London, 2007).

Elain Harwood, *Chamberlin Powell & Bon,* (London, 2012).

David Heathcote, *Barbican: Penthouse over the City,* (London, 2004).

Nicholas Kenyon (ed.), *The City of London: Architectural Tradition & Innovation in the Square Mile,* (London, 2011).

Alan Powers, *Britain: Modern Architectures in History* (London, 2007).

Richard Trench, *London before the Blitz,* (London, 1989).

Chronology

AD 200	The Romans erect a wall around their settlement, Londinium. The site that will become known as Barbican lies just beyond it on the north side.
1090	St Giles' Cripplegate church is founded.
1664–6	The Great Plague decimates the population in the area.
1666	The Great Fire ravages London but most of the Barbican area escapes.
1851	The City's resident population is over 125,000 of which 14,000 in the ward of Cripplegate. It is the centre of the rag trade.
29 Dec 1940	One night of intense bombing reduces the area that is now the Barbican to cinders.
1943–4	Plans for the reconstruction of London are made. John H. Forshaw and Patrick Abercrombie prepare the 'County of London Plan' and then the 'Greater London Plan'. These address London's traffic congestion problems and propose to reduce the population by building new satellite towns.
1947	William G. Holford and Charles H. Holden produce a reconstruction plan for the Corporation of London, the 'City of London Plan'. According to this plan, the City is to be rebuilt principally as a commercial area with a small residential population.
1951	Only 5,324 people live in the City and 48 in the ward of Cripplegate.
1952	Geoffry Powell wins the competition launched by the Corporation of London to build the Golden Lane Estate. Chamberlin, Powell & Bon is established.
1953–4	The campaign to develop the Barbican area begins.
Jun 1955	CPB submit their first report investigating the possibility of providing housing in the City on the Barbican site.
May 1956	CPB submit their second report on the Barbican redevelopment to the Court of Common Council.

Aug 1956	The Minister of Housing and Local Government, Duncan Sandys, supports the idea that the Barbican should be developed as a residential neighbourhood and the recommendation is accepted by the City the following year.
Apr 1959	CPB submit their third report on the redevelopment of the Barbican site, Barbican Redevelopment 1959, to the Court of Common Council which approves it.
May 1960	CPB are appointed architects for the buildings and the master plan of the Barbican.
1962	CPB are instructed to draw up new proposals separating the Guildhall School from the arts centre so that the latter's theatre and concert hall can be used full-time by professional companies.
1963	Building begins on the main scheme including residential blocks and the City of London School for Girls which is completed in 1969.
1965–6	The Corporation of the City of London invite the Royal Shakespeare Company and the London Symphony Orchestra to take up a permanent residency at the arts centre.
1966	Building work is suspended for a year due to strike action.
1968	The first residential block, Speed House, is completed. Tenants move in in 1969. CPB submit their report on the arts centre to the Court of Common Council.
1971–7	Construction of the Guildhall School of Music and Drama.
1971–82	Construction of the arts centre.
Mar 1982	The Barbican Centre is inaugurated by Queen Elizabeth II.
1993–5	Theo Crosby of Pentagram Design and Polly Hope make some modifications to the Barbican Centre.
2001	The Barbican complex is listed as a Grade II building.
2005–7	The Barbican Centre is refurbished by Allford Hall Monaghan Morris who give it a new entrance at street level on Silk Street and remodel the Foyer.

Acknowledgements

Barbican: Life, History, Architecture is indebted to many individuals who have been exceptionally generous with their knowledge. John Honer, former partner of CPB (Barbican), spent many hours discussing the Barbican and sharing his documentation – he could not have been more helpful. Polly Powell, Geoffry Powell's daughter, opened her archives and proved extremely supportive of the project from start to finish. Diana Flanagan, Jean Chamberlin's niece, and her husband Robert recalled Jean and Joe Chamberlin and Christof Bon, bringing them to life. Frank Woods, former partner of CPB, guided us through the archives of CPB and showed us rare drawings by Chamberlin.

Tom Dixon, Mike Leigh, Jonathan Meades, Eric Parry and Vivienne Westwood contributed inspiring texts about the Barbican for which we are most grateful. We are also indebted to Otto Saumarez Smith for his scholarly contribution to the book.

Meeting with scholars, residents of the Barbican and architects was undoubtedly one of the most enjoyable parts of the research and we would like to extend our warmest thanks to: Elain Harwood, expert of Chamberlin, Powell & Bon's work; Eva Branscome, Sophie Leighton-Kelly, Jilly MacLeod and Ken Powell who shared their knowledge and research about the Barbican; Barbican residents Daniel Edwards and John and Jan McLean, who conveyed their passion for the estate; and Greg Penoyre of Penoyre & Prasad LLP and Peter Inskip of Peter Inskip + Peter Jenkins Architects who offered their insights into the Barbican.

At the Barbican, we would like to thank Steff Langley, Nicholas Triantafyllou and Sidd Khajuria for their photographs as well as Nozomi Miike for her invaluable picture research.

Picture credits

Every effort has been made to contact copyright holders for their permission to reproduce material in this book. The publishers will endeavour to correct in following editions any errors or omissions that are brought to their attention.

Cover photography: Sue Barr/ Construction Photography/Photoshot

Architectural Press Archive/RIBA Library Photographs Collection: top 14, 50, 59, top 68, 86-7.

Courtesy of the Barbican: 77.

Photo © Sue Barr: right 72, 73.

Felix Clay: left 83.

Photography by Alfred Cracknell: top 50, bottom 51.

Diana Flanagan: top 37.

© FLC/ADAGP, Paris and DACS, London 2014: top 13.

John Honer: Former Partner CPB (Barbican): bottom 37, 42, 43.

Siddharth Khajuria: 61, 88–9.

Rebecca Langley: 75.

Steff Langley: 4–5, 8, 9, bottom 13, 17, 22–3, 27, 29, 77, bottom 82, 84, 84–85.

London Metropolitan Archives, City of London, SC/GL/BAD/001: 30.

London Metropolitan Archives, City of London: 32.

John Maltby/RIBA Library Photographs Collection: 33, 58, bottom 68, 80–1.

Tom Mannion: 69, 70.

Lee Mawdsley: 35, bottom 87.

© Museum of London/By Kind Permission of The Commissioner of the City of London Police: 31.

Photo copyright Jane Northcote: left 72.

© Neil Perry: bottom 14, 71.

Polly Powell: bottom left 39, 40, 41.

Polly Powell, © FLC/ADAGP, Paris and DACS, London 2014: top 39.

RIBA Library Drawings & Archives Collection: 18–19, 52, 54, 55, 56, 57, top 87.

RIBA Library Drawings & Archives Collection/By permission of the Gordon Cullen Estate: 24–5, 53.

RIBA Library Photographs Collection, courtesy of The Architects' Journal: bottom right 39.

Andrew Ridley Photography (www. aridleyphotography.com): top 82.

Photo by India Roper-Evans: 79.

Harry Todd/Getty Images: top 51.

Nicholas Triantafyllou: 2-3, 10–1, 21, 45, right 83.

Courtesy of Twyford Bathrooms: bottom 63.

First published 2014 by Barbican Centre

Barbican Centre
Silk Street
London EC2Y 8DS
Barbican.org.uk

All texts by Anna Ferrari unless otherwise stated.

Editors: Jane Alison and Anna Ferrari
Book design and layout: Peter Dawson, Namkwan Cho www.gradedesign.com
Copy edited by: Ariella Yedgar
Printed by: The Kingsbury Press

ISBN 978-0-946372-41-6

The City of London
Corporation is the founder
and principal funder
of the Barbican Centre